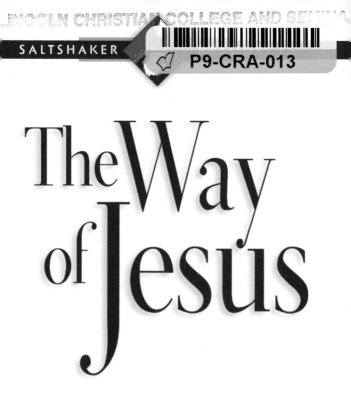

The Way of Jesus

Rebecca Manley Pippert

InterVarsity Press
Downers Grove, Illinois
Leicester, England

InterVarsity Press
P.O. Box 1400, Downers Grove, IL 60515-1426
World Wide Web: www.ivpress.com
E-mail: mail@ivpress.com

Inter-Varsity Press, England
38 De Montfort Street, Leicester LE1 7GP, England
World Wide Web: www.ivpbooks.com
E-mail: ivp@uccf.org.uk

InterVarsity Press® is the book-publishing division of InterVarsity Christian Fellowship/USA®, a student movement active on campus at hundreds of universities, colleges and schools of nursing in the United States of America, and a member movement of the International Fellowship of Evangelical Students. For information about local and regional activities, write Public Relations Dept., InterVarsity Christian Fellowship/USA, 6400 Schroeder Rd., P.O. Box 7895, Madison, WI 53707-7895, or visit the IVCF website at <www.ivcf.org>.

Inter-Varsity Press, England, is the book-publishing division of the Universities and Colleges Christian Fellowship (formerly the Inter-Varsity Fellowship), a student movement linking Christian Unions in universities and colleges throughout the United Kingdom and the Republic of Ireland, and a member movement of the International Fellowship of Evangelical Students. For information about local and national activities write to UCCF, 38 De Montfort Street, Leicester LE1 7GP.

Cover design: Cindy Kiple

Cover and interior image: Michael Busselle/Getty Images

U.S. ISBN 0-8308-2124-4

U.K. ISBN 0-85111-791-0

Printed in the United States of America ∞

P	17	16	15	14	13	12	11	10	9	8	7	6	5	4	3	2	1
Y	16	15	14	13	12	11	10	09	08	07	06	05	04	.03			

To Ruth Siemens,

My mentor, my friend and

a true hero of the faith,

whose life has shaped not only mine

but countless others around the world.

I dedicate this series to you—

with gratitude beyond expression.

111490

Once I had the opportunity of auditing courses for a year at Harvard. One day one of my professors said to me, "Becky, I am fascinated by the fact that you're such a committed Christian. I'm an atheist myself, but I've always wanted to ask a serious Christian a few questions. Would you mind?"

"Certainly," I said.

"My first question is this: In the end, isn't life the same, whether you believe in Jesus or not? Don't all of us long to make meaning out of life? Don't all of us want to find identity? Don't all of us want to be loved? Isn't the stuff of what makes us human the same whether we believe in God or not?"

I said, "Yes, that is true. Being a believer doesn't give us an exemption card from life. We all experience the issues you mention, whether we believe in God or not."

"All right, then," he said, "let me ask you a second question: Isn't life difficult whether you believe in Jesus or not? Don't Christians struggle with bankruptcy and illness? Don't we all try to raise our children the best we know how? And if they fail, don't we suffer terribly?"

"Life is very difficult," I replied. "In fact, I think there may be even more challenges for a serious follower of Jesus. Yes, life is very difficult whether you believe in Jesus or not."

He said, "All right, let me ask you the third question: Don't Christians fail? I grant you that you may do better in some areas than the rest of us do, but I have met some born-again Christians who were racists, who were proud and self-righteous—and don't say, 'Oh well, then they couldn't have been real Christians.'"

I said, "No, I'm not going to say that. Yes, we fail as you fail."

He said, "There you have it. If life is the same, if life is difficult and if you fail like we fail, then Jesus doesn't really make a difference. Your answers proved it. Maybe Jesus is like a hot water bottle that gets you through the night—you have your fix, I have mine—but Jesus doesn't intrinsically make a difference."

Does Jesus Truly Make a Difference in Our Lives?

While I do not agree with the professor's conclusion, he does hit the nail on the head when he asks if Jesus truly makes a difference in our lives. If he does, where is the evidence? What is especially confusing for people is when they see the church imitating the world at its worst. One skeptic friend said recently, "I get so tired of turning my Sunday TV dial and hearing a gospel message that sounds more like a beer commercial. 'Just name the name of Jesus and claim that Mercedes! Get all the gusto you need with Jesus!' It sounds more like the gospel according to Trump."

It is equally confusing when seekers hear a prophetic word coming not from the devout but from the secular corner. Ellen Goodman of the *Boston Globe* once did a piece titled "The Goodness of Guilt." The late Meg Greenfield of *Newsweek* did an article titled "The Possibilities of Moral Absolutes." Dan Rather once did a radio spot called "Whatever Happened to Sin?" Ted Koppel, in his now celebrated commencement address at Duke University, said, "We actually live in an age in which we think slogans will save us: 'Shoot up if you must, just use a clean needle.' 'Enjoy sex whenever and with whomever, just use a condom.'" He said, "No, the answer is no. And it's not because it isn't cool or isn't smart, or because you might end up dying in an AIDS ward. It is no, because it is wrong. We have spent five thousand years as a race of rational human beings trying to drag ourselves out of the primeval slime in our search for truth and moral absolutes."

"In the final analysis," Koppel said, "truth is not a polite tap on the shoulder. It is a howling reproach. What Moses brought down from Mount Sinai were not the 'Ten Suggestions.' "

No wonder people are confused. While political and social pundits and researchers are discovering that members of the Boomer generation are searching for moral authority, some preachers are throwing theirs away.

Let me ask it again: Does Jesus Christ make a difference? The Jesus of Scripture certainly insists that he does. While other religious leaders pointed attention away from themselves, Jesus calls attention to himself. He claims to forgive sins. He says he has always existed and that one day he will return to judge the world at the end of time. He not only talks as if he were God, he boldly proclaims, "I am the resurrection and the life. . . . Whoever lives and believes in me will never die" (John 11:25-26). In short, Jesus insists that if our desire is to find joy, peace and inner transformation that lasts forever; to be connected to God and to others; and to find meaning for our anxious lives—if it is real change we are after—then he's our man.

Facing the Mess

Whether we find such claims preposterous or worth considering, the interesting caveat is the condition necessary for experiencing the change that Jesus offers. In order to experience the miracle and the mystery of the radical change that Jesus brings, we have to face the mess. What is the mess? The Bible makes the rather rude assertion that *we* are the mess. The mess is the human heart. The mess is a word that has little cash value in our politically correct age: *sin.* The British writer G. K. Chesterton said, "I find it amazing that moderns reject the doctrine of original sin when it is the only Christian doctrine that can be empirically verified."

Hold on, we protest. Surely you don't expect a twenty-first-century person to believe that human woes could be tied to something as archaic as the notion of sin? Nobody believes that anymore. In fact, since the time of the Enlightenment we have not even used the concept of sin as means for understanding the human condition.

Yet the notion of human fallenness is now recapturing our attention as we struggle to understand terrorist attacks, mass murders and reports of children murdering children. Literary thinkers such as Albert Camus and William Golding, author of *Lord of the Flies,* have grappled with the dark side of human nature. It was precisely Karl Menniger's point in *Whatever Happened to Sin?* We are suffering from some disease, but we have lost the category to even identify the problem. We are sinners with no name for it. Ernest Becker, the Pulitzer Prize-winning social psychologist who wrote *The Denial of Death,* states that the plight of the modern person is that he or she is "a sinner with no word for it." Becker, who is not a self-described believer, even characterizes the disease as a disharmony with others—individuals creating their own worlds from within themselves, inflating their own importance, refusing to admit their cosmic dependence. So perhaps we are not dealing with something as ridiculous and outdated as we thought. Perhaps the Bible's candor has done us a service by not only addressing the problem but giving us a name for it.

Do We Recognize the Problem?

Assuming for the moment that what ails us is the disease of sin, even before we define sin from a biblical perspective, we still need to ask two questions.

First, does our culture help us to see that the problem plaguing us is sin? I think it's very clear that it does not. In Western society, and in America in particular, we have a remarkably naive, Boy-Scout approach to understanding human nature. We think we're basically wonderful people who occasionally do bad deeds. So we're shocked by sin when instead we should be staggered by grace.

It hasn't always been this way. The framers who wrote the Constitution, while not necessarily all Christians, had a much more ruggedly realistic understanding of human nature. They understood that human nature, while reflecting God's image, was still deeply flawed. But such an understanding of human nature is not common in America today.

Second, does the church understand that the problem plaguing us is sin? Christians certainly know that Jesus came to save sinners. But when pressed, do they really understand the distinction between being sinners and being mildly neurotic? I believe our cultural denial of sin has affected the believer almost as much as it has affected the skeptic.

This truth came home to me at Harvard in a psychology class. The professor asked us to break up into small groups. "I want you to share with one another what problems you are experiencing," he told us, "and how some of the psychological principles we've been studying could help you." The honesty of these students in acknowledging real problems was very moving. What was even more poignant was their difficulty in finding answers to their problems.

Upon leaving the psychology class that day, I went across campus to a Bible study. The difference between those two groups could not have been more exaggerated. Why? No one in the Bible study ever acknowledged having a problem. I heard people sincerely praising the Lord and sharing meaningful Bible verses. But nobody was willing to share a problem or to admit weakness. Well, that's not quite true. Let me put it this way: the only people who were identified as having problems were the ones who hadn't shown up but who were "struggling and needed prayer!"

As I walked out of the Bible study, I asked myself, *What is the difference between that secular Harvard class and the Christian Bible study?* I realized it was that the secular psychology class had all of the problems and none of the answers, while the Christian Bible study had all the answers but none of the problems!

What does it sound like when a group of people, no matter how sincere, speak as if they've got all the answers but none of the problems? It sounds like "happy talk"—hearty, hale, but not quite believable. It's not believable because it is a form of denial. If I had confidentially asked a Bible study member how he was really doing, I suspect he might have answered, "Well, I see God's will, purpose and promises in Scripture, and I see the reality of my own life. Frankly, in some areas of my life there's a gap, but I feared it would be unspiritual to admit it." But did Jesus ever suggest that genuine conversion produced instantaneously "finished products?" He said, rather, that true spirituality begins by admitting where the gaps lie and turning to God for help.

Because our culture denies the reality of sin, I fear that Christians fall into the trap of feeling that it is a sin to admit they are sinners. Yet for skeptic and believer alike, the cross reveals that our secret is out. The message of the cross is clear: if Jesus had to die, then human beings have a problem that they need to own.

Owning Our Sin

Now we come to the crux of the problem. The Bible says that we can't benefit from the cure that Christ offers unless we understand the nature of the disease. But in order to understand the nature of our disease, we must first acknowledge that we have a disease.

I have a friend who is a recovering alcoholic. I asked him once how he came to faith after many years of battling alcoholism. He said, "It all started the day a Christian friend came to my home and took me to his Alcoholics Anonymous meeting. It was an unusual group because all the members were committed Christians. But Becky, when I walked into the room, I knew instantly I was in the presence of people who had suffered. They put their arms around me, and they said, 'Bob, you've got a problem. You're responsible for it, but you can't overcome it without the help of God. But we will stand with you and walk with you, and we will see you through this.' As I walked out of that room, I said to myself, 'You have been in the presence of the wounded and the healed.'"

"Bob," I said, "that is the best description of the church I have ever heard. We have a problem—it's called sin. We must own it. We are responsible for it, but we can't conquer it apart from the power of God. Each Sunday we sit with fellow pilgrims who share the same problem and seek the same cure."

He looked at me, smiled, and said, "Let me tell you what it was like the first time I ever went to church as a drunk. The message was polite but firm—come back when you have your act together; we will have no unpleasantness here."

I asked, "Then why isn't the church more like an AA meeting?"

Bob replied, "Because there are some of us who really don't believe that the rot is in us too. We may sing hymns, we may praise Jesus, but do we really know why Jesus died *for us*? Or do we just say to ourselves, 'I may have a few problems, but I'm not as bad as those guys over there.' Not until we own our sin can our faith deepen and our experience of grace be profound."

What am I saying? Do we have to become alcoholics in order to understand the true nature of our problem? No, of course not. What *is* necessary is that we understand and own our problem. But how do we do that, especially when psychologists are quick to remind us that we are the "hiding species"? While dogs and cats do not have a problem with denial, it seems to be our specialty. Where do we go to gain insight into the nature of our problem? I believe that all patterns of denial fall away at the foot of the cross. There are two central images we need to keep in mind when we ponder the meaning of the cross. First, *Jesus died, and we crucified him.* Second, *Jesus died, and we were crucified with him.*

Jesus died, and we crucified him. In the New Testament book of Acts it says, "[Jesus] was handed over to you by God's set purpose and foreknowledge; and you, with the help of wicked men, put him to death by nailing him to the cross" (Acts 2:23). But what does that mean? How could we possibly be responsible for the death of someone who died two thousand years ago?

Let's look at this for a moment from a biblical perspective. According to the Bible, all of us suffer from the disease of sin. Jesus made it clear that his purpose in coming was to resolve the crisis of sin by dying on the cross. He didn't die merely for those who were alive at the time, but for all sinners and for all times—yesterday, today and until the close of human history. If Christ is who he says he is, and if his sacrifice on the cross was necessitated by the problem of sin that we all share, then whether we were there pounding the nails or not, we are still responsible. The brokenness and woundedness we see within ourselves and around us is precisely what led Christ to the cross.

You may say, "Well, thanks but no thanks. I didn't ask Jesus to do this for me. That was his choice, not mine." And you would be right. It *was* God's choice to send his son to our planet and, through the mystery of the sacrifice of the cross, to offer us a bridge back to God. We may flatly reject it. But if we choose to benefit from what his death accomplished, we must acknowledge that it was our sin—as well as the sin of the whole planet—that led Christ to the cross.

Viewing Sin in Light of the Cross

I once met a woman at a conference where I was speaking who was terribly distressed. "Ten years ago," she told me, "my fiancé (now her husband) and I were the youth ministers of a large, thriving church. The adults loved and esteemed us. We helped all kinds of young people spiritually." She said, "But during our last year of ministry in that church, we began to have sexual relations." She continued, "You can't imagine the spiritual schizophrenia we felt, knowing we were compromising in one of the primary areas we were trying to help the youth with. It was horrible. But then I discovered I was pregnant. Becky, for us to have gone to this church and told them I was pregnant was unthinkable."

I asked, "Why?"

She replied, "There had never been any scandal in that church." (At least there was no scandal that she knew of!) Then she added, "But I have to be honest. The other reason I couldn't confess was my pride. For them to discover that I wasn't who they thought I was seemed unbearable. So I did the only thing I felt was an option. I had an abortion. My wedding day was the worst day of my whole life. I walked down the aisle and saw everybody smiling at me, and I said to myself, *You're a murderer. You have murdered an innocent life, and they may look at you and smile, but God knows, and you know, what you're like. You are a murderer.*"

The young woman continued, "Becky, it's been ten years. My husband has experienced the forgiveness of God. But I don't know where to go with my guilt because all I keep saying to myself is, *How could you have done it? How could you have murdered an innocent life? How could you do it?*"

She was so desperate that I knew I needed God's immediate help. So I silently prayed, "Lord, give me a word for this woman." As I prayed I felt the Spirit of God give me a message for her. But as I was mustering up courage to speak, she kept saying one thing over and over again: "How could I have been capable of murdering an innocent life?"

I took a deep breath and said, "My dear friend, I don't understand why you're so surprised. This isn't the first death of an innocent that you are responsible for—it's your second. Don't you see that the cross shows all of us as crucifiers—aborters or nonaborters, religious or atheists alike. All of us are responsible for the death of the only true innocent who ever lived. It wasn't murder, though. Jesus gave his life as a gift. But do you think there is any sin you've committed that didn't nail Jesus to the cross? Martin Luther said, 'We carry his very nails in our pockets.' If you have done it before, what makes you think you couldn't be responsible for the death of a lesser innocent? I'm surprised that you're surprised."

She stopped crying. "You're right," she said, "my sin drove Jesus to the cross. I've just realized something—I have felt more guilt over the death of my own son than the death of God's Son. But Becky, I came to you saying I've done the worst thing imaginable, and you tell me that I've actually done something worse than that?" (I admit, this does not exactly qualify as the greatest counseling technique!) Then she said, "But Becky, if the cross shows me that I'm worse than I had imagined, it also shows me my sin has been absorbed and forgiven. If the worst thing any human can do is to be responsible for the death of Jesus, and *that* can be forgiven, how can anything else not be forgiven?" With tears streaming down her face she said, "Oh, Becky, talk about amazing grace!"

That day I saw a woman transformed by a new understanding of the meaning of the cross. The paradox of the cross is that it highlights our worst in order to leave us absolutely no doubt that whatever we have done can be forgiven. The cross obeys the greatest law of acceptance, and that is this: in order to know I've been accepted, I've got to know I've been accepted at my worst. That means no one can ever say, "Oh, I know all this talk about how much God loves me. But if God really knew me . . ." The message of God from the cross is, "Oh, I know you, and you're in a lot worse shape than you even know. And it's going to be all right, because my Son died for you. Receive my gift; receive my love."

Think about it: God is willing to forgive us for the death of Christ. What sin will we ever confess that could be more grievous than that? If God is willing to forgive us the worst sin, then why wouldn't God forgive the lesser sins? That is why we can bring our sins to the cross in freedom, even in the context of joy, because God's solution is so wonderful! Jesus died, we crucified him, and there is nothing that cannot be forgiven—except for one thing. What is that? It is the sin of insisting that we are not sinners—which is, in fact, the very disease of modernity. The disease of the modern age says, "I don't have a problem. I'm innocent." That denial of sin is the one thing God can't forgive.

How can God forgive what we insist is not a problem? To insist we are sinless not only negates the necessity of Christ's sacrifice, but it's refusing God's gift of the Holy Spirit, who indwells us permanently when we place our trust in Christ. Why would we need God's *Holy* Spirit to reside in us when we assume are sinless?

Jesus died, we crucified him, and apart from insisting on our innocence, there is nothing that cannot be forgiven.

Jesus died, and we were crucified with him. In the New Testament book of Galatians, the apostle Paul writes, "I have been crucified with Christ, and I no longer live, but Christ lives in me" (Galatians 2:20). But what does he mean? Paul tells us that he has wonderful news: everyone who is alive in Christ is dead! As we read this, it's tempting to think, *Well, maybe Paul was just having a bad day.*

But Paul would no doubt answer us, "If you only knew *what* Jesus put to death when he died on the cross, you would rise in hymns of praise!"

What is so wrong with us that it necessitated the death of Jesus? I mean, we're not that bad. Most of us don't rob banks or abuse children or embezzle money. What exactly is this disease of sin? We need to answer this question before we examine what it means to say we have been "crucified with Christ."

A Name for It

In the eighth century B.C. the Old Testament prophet Ezekiel correctly diagnosed our disease: "You are a man and not a god, though you think you are as wise as a god" (Ezekiel 28:3). Brazilian psychiatrist Norberto Keppe says it is "the disease of theomania—the desire to be god, . . . the desire to be the playwright instead of the actor in the drama." In theological shorthand, all humans suffer from having a "god-complex." We keep getting ourselves and God mixed up. We keep thinking we're in charge, and we actually pretend that we are our own God. Instead of bowing before a sovereign God, we appoint ourselves as managers of God's universe. Sin isn't an isolated act of wrong behavior. It can't be summed up by the old adage "I don't smoke, drink, dance or chew or go with girls who do." Sin is refusing to let God be God. It is embracing an addiction to ourselves.

And here is the shocker: we can't do anything about it. There aren't four simple steps that will transform us from self-centered to God-centered. That is only something God can do, and that is something God *did* through Christ's death on the cross.

What happens when we put our faith and trust in Christ? We begin to experience what he secured for us on the cross. When the Bible tells us that Christ died for us, it means the backbone of our rebellion, this hopeless mire of prideful, rebellious self-centeredness, has been nailed to the cross with Christ. That doesn't mean our "god-complex" was totally eradicated, but at some fundamental level our sin nature was crushed. Yes, we will have to defeat sin day by day as we walk with Jesus. But without the cross we would not have the freedom to choose anything *other* than sin. The cross bought us our freedom! Now we can learn to live in sync with God's Spirit and his ways.

British author C. S. Lewis, in his book *Mere Christianity,* has a wonderful way of describing life with Christ. "Christianity," he wrote, "is not like teaching a horse to jump better and better." You see, that remedy is moralism and legalism— which makes us nice, but it doesn't make us new.

Rather, Lewis concluded that Christianity is "like turning a horse into a winged creature . . . [so] it will soar over fences which could never have been jumped."

Jesus died, and we crucified him. Never underestimate sin when it cost Jesus his life. Yet never forget that there is nothing that cannot be forgiven, except the sin of insisting we are not sinners.

Jesus died, and we were crucified with him. Don't overestimate sin either. You're freer than you know. Rise and walk in the freedom of your new God-centered nature, given to those who put their faith in Christ.

Where It All Began

But if our problem is sin and it was God who created us, where did our problem originate? First let's look at what God's intentions were for the human race. The Bible begins the diagnosis by telling us what the healthy organism looks like. It shows us what we were created to be, what happened to change us and what the consequences have been. To understand what it says, we will take a look at the familiar biblical story of creation (which shows us who we were intended to be) and the story of the Fall (which shows us who we have become). Together, these stories give us the right framework and the right categories for understanding what it means to be human, including what is normal and what is abnormal, what is the source of our true happiness and what is the cause of our problems.

What did God intend when he created the human race? According to the story of Adam and Eve, human beings were created by a good God and made in his image and likeness. He made a universe that is interrelated, interdependent and integrated with God at the center. The Bible tells us that God created us in love. And in love God also gave us the gift of freedom—the freedom to love, to reason, to create, to be unique and diverse, yet crowned with moral perfection, and so to live in harmony with God and the rest of his creation. Here creature and Creator knew real bliss. Our nature was good, though different from that of our Creator. Being made finite, dependent and not self-sufficient, we were to be fulfilled in God. Being made in his image, we were made to love and be loved, to trust and know protection, to know and be known, to live in joy and experience delight. God made us with these desires, and he intended to fulfill them. Thus the path to freedom and fulfillment comes when we live as we were created to be: in harmony with the center of all life—God—not simply centered on ourselves.

What went wrong? As Pascal said, "Certainly nothing offends us more rudely than the doctrine of Original Sin, yet without this mystery, the most incomprehensible of all, we are incomprehensible to ourselves." The story of Adam and Eve reveals not only the marvel of creation but also what went wrong. The Bible tells us that at some point humans revolted by asserting their will over their Creator. In defiance and arrogance (and stupidity) they tried to be equal with God. They wanted to call the shots. They refused to trust themselves to God's love. In not making God their center, they disobeyed him and contradicted the laws of their own nature. They misused their freedom and chose to be centered in themselves instead of centered in God.

How did Adam and Eve react once their guilt was discovered? Not too well. Adam sets the human race off on its grand process of denial by pathetically attempting to deny there is a problem at all and hiding from God. It's as if he thinks that if he can escape getting caught, then maybe it did not really happen. Then, once discovered, his next line of defense is blame: "That woman—she gave it to me." And then he adds a final touch: "The woman *you* gave me, Lord." From denial through blame to rationalization, his argument runs like this: *If God cannot pick me a better partner, how can it be my fault?* And his reactions are so smooth and deftly developed that one would never guess he was a rookie at the business of sin.

The story of Adam and Eve was written thousands of years ago, long before our therapeutic age. Yet it describes their reactions toward their rebellion against God in terms of what we now know as classic character defenses (denial, scapegoating and so on). But the Bible makes it clear that these are merely guilt-laden reactions to the problem. They are not the problem itself.

What were the consequences of sin entering the world? What was the result of the decision to strike out and seek independence? Nothing remained the same. From that point on, all human relationships became distorted—with God, with nature, with one another and with themselves. Sin came in and touched their existence on every level. It reached beyond personal struggles with pride, envy, greed and lust. Evil spread to every level of creation from the micro to the macro: oppression, injustice and mistreatment of the widow, the orphan and the alien. Even the greed of a few individuals can bring down entire corporations, causing thousands of people to lose their jobs. Another result of sin's rupture of our relationship with God is fear and anxiety, traits all conscious creatures share. And why are we anxious?

Because sin means we need to be God but aren't.

From Adam and Eve to us. Thus the Bible calls our problem *sin* and locates it at the very center of human personality. In essence, *sin is the deliberate claim to the right to ourselves and the equally deliberate refusal to worship God as God.* The story of Adam and Eve is therefore our story too. We may not have chosen so consciously to rebel, but we are rebels nonetheless. We too have made self the center and source of life in place of God. It is that same rebellion against God that causes us to use these psychological defenses that keep us from seeing the truth about ourselves. The problem with humanity, the Bible says bluntly, is not a metaphysical problem (in other words, a design problem in our very being, which could be blamed on our Creator). It is inescapably a moral problem, and it is our fault.

This means that life as we currently experience it is not the way it was created to be. We are living on a planet that is in a state of dysfunction. Suffering, sorrow, disease and death are all around us, but it wasn't meant to be so! Indeed, there was a time it was *not* so, when justice reigned, when harmony and love existed and were untainted. But we now live on a planet that is subject to evil.

Since evil is a moral and not a metaphysical problem, it is abnormal and not normal. Death was not a part of God's plan when he created us. The abnormality of sin gives death a sting, which explains the outrage we feel when loved ones die prematurely. There is something terribly wrong about the way things are. Sin has come into the picture. Human rebellion has altered the very structure of reality. But God is not responsible for the mess. In fact, as we see at the cross, it is his desire to deal with it once and for all.

But Is Sin So Serious?

Perhaps you're still wondering why God makes such a big deal about sin. Okay, you say, maybe humans are responsible for sin entering this planet. But after all, we can forgive our own excesses. We don't get that upset over everything we do. We manage to forgive and forget—so why can't God loosen up a bit? He sounds pretty uptight. Who wants to spend time with somebody who can't relax and let bygones be bygones?

Just imagine for a moment that you are God. Imagine the picture you had in mind as you created planet earth. Your desire, I would bet, was that your human creatures should live in harmony with you and one another. But then imagine that the universe *you created* chose not to go your way. Human beings decided, in other words, that they didn't want you to be the center of their existence. So you've been compelled to watch generation after generation, century after century, as people pollute and destroy nature, nations, one another and themselves.

You're now watching the entire globe at war. You see that humans use the gifts you gave them—intelligence and imagination, tools that were created for good purpose—to destroy one another. You see human brilliance and skill used so fiendishly as to defy comprehension. You watch the Crusades carried out *in your name*. You see the Holocaust—human beings shoveling the children of other human beings into gas chambers, using babies for target practice. You see bright, alert, young minds drugging themselves into oblivion. You watch them laboring earnestly to create tools that will obliterate the planet. But does your creation pause to think, let alone weep and kneel and ask forgiveness? On the contrary, we blame *you*.

No big deal, did someone say? The wonder is not that God takes sin so seriously but that he takes us even more seriously—so much so that he was willing to pay the ultimate price to have sin dealt with.

Treating the Disease of Sin

"All right," we say, "I get the point. Clearly this planet has gotten itself in a mess. And it may be true that the core of the problem is our choice to put ourselves, not God, at the center." Maybe we even respond by saying, "I do recognize that I keep trying to run the show. And although I would never have seen it on my own, if there is a God in the universe, then I am a moral rebel. But I am tired of the confusion and hollowness, the lack of purpose. So what can I do? Just tell me what to do to remedy the situation, and I'll do it."

But first we need to face the practical results of our insistence on playing God. Sin has left us hopelessly addicted to ourselves. We were created to be centered in God, and instead, we are hopelessly centered in ourselves. What can we do to transform our self-centeredness, our continual insistence on running the show? How do we defeat our self-absorption? The Bible's response is startling. Absolutely nothing! We can't reach in and straighten a twisted nature. We simply lack the power. If we are to be restored to what we were intended to be, it will have to be done for us.

But wait a minute. Now we are told we are responsible for a condition that we are powerless to change. How can we be responsible for something that we have no power to change?

Curiously, the problem of addiction sheds light on this complex paradox of responsibility and powerlessness, especially as it relates to change. Why? Because the path of recovery for all addicts lies in first admitting their powerlessness. They no longer deny that they have a problem. They know that help must come from the outside. Their only choice is whether they will seek that help from a source beyond themselves. They alone are responsible for that choice. No one else can make the decision for them.

Exactly the same is true of sin. We are responsible for our condition, but we are powerless to change it. Only help from outside ourselves—the help of God—can change us. But it is up to us whether we seek such a solution. So long as we still "hold out," thinking that our happiness depends on someone else changing, waiting for an emotionally distant parent to transform magically or for some circumstance to alter, we will never get well. So long as we entertain any notion that our problems will be solved by someone else doing what we think they should, we doom ourselves to despair.

Here is where we decisively part company with our culture. Our culture tells us to ignore our self-doubts and to feel only positive thoughts about ourselves. But I am saying the opposite. Pay attention to those lurking doubts. Listen closely to that nagging discontent. Yes, it is important to have a healthy self-esteem. But ironically, the best road to health faces the reality of the sickness. Those who want wholeness, love and meaning for their lives must face the worst first. It is only in giving up on ourselves that we can go beyond ourselves and find ourselves.

So what are we to do if we cannot overcome our self-addiction by sheer willpower? The truth is we can't practice four steps that free us to be God-centered instead of self-centered. Only a power that is stronger than ourselves can help us overcome ourselves. That is something only God can do, and that is something that God did.

What does the Bible offer as a plan of treatment for our condition? Here is where the words of Jesus begin to make sense. Jesus called his message "good news" because help is at hand. He knew that the fatal disease within human nature could only be cured by the Divine Surgeon. Our only hope for remedy is if God does something. And according to Jesus, he has.

The Mystery of the Cross

Both the remedy and the proof of the love behind God's act are seen most compellingly in the cross. The mystery of the cross is literally the crux of the Christian faith. It did not make sense to the disciples initially, and I doubt if it will ever make sense to us. How can the death of God's Son make sick people well or sinful people forgiven? To many that sounds like mumbo-jumbo. Yet the message is unmistakable: Only in the cross, however hidden, is there any means of deliverance, of wholeness and of peace. Only in what looks like a dead-end do we have the hope of a new start.

The paradoxes of the cross lead us to ask the ethical question frequently posed by skeptics: "How can a God who is truly good forgive what is truly bad without morally compromising himself?" Everyone reflecting on a divine solution to the human predicament should wrestle with that question. How can God change the heart of an estranged humanity and enable us to be reconciled and "at one" with him without self-compromise? For example, how can God reconcile the opposing demands of his justice, which must judge evil, and his love, which wants to save the evildoer? How can God forgive without compromising his holiness, and judge evil without frustrating his love? How can he forgive wrong without moral compromise, and love without being angry over what destroys us?

That raises another problem. We tend to be taken aback by the thought that God could be angry. How can a deity who is perfect and loving ever be angry? Just look at us—we manage to be very understanding and accepting of our flaws. We take pride in our tolerance of the excesses of others. So what is God's problem? What sort of a God gets angry? Of course, the Bible never suggests that God's anger is lightly provoked. Or that God is ready to pounce at the first misstep. On the contrary, we are told he is "slow to anger" (Exodus 34:6). Nor does his anger come from having a bad temper. Indeed, God's anger issues from the intensity and depth of his love for us, as well as the height of his moral perfection and his outrage against evil. Nor is God's anger a kind that comes from feeling slighted or ignored, as in "You've really hurt my feelings this time." God's anger is a just anger and from perfect motives.

Our problem in pondering anything about God is that we bring our human pettiness, jealousies and problems into the analysis. We can't help that, but it makes it difficult to imagine God having emotions similar to ours without the pollution ours bring. Even so, it may help to examine a comparable form of human anger. Think of how we feel when we see someone we love ravaged by unwise actions or relationships. Do we respond with benign tolerance as we might toward strangers? Far from it. We are dead against whatever is destroying the one we love.

Loving people with an addiction is a good example. It is one of the most frustrating, infuriating experiences many of us ever go through. I have seen bright, talented people who, because of the effects of drugs, are unable to remember conversations that took place mere hours ago. I have seen someone so frantic to get to a bathroom to snort cocaine that they nearly knocked me over to get there. I have watched their noses drip and listened to their self-inflated, drug-induced statements. And in their drugged deception, they were convinced they were acting normally. To this day, I don't think they are aware that I knew what was going on. If they were, they would say it was a gross exaggeration. They were in total control, they thought. Their use of drugs was just "recreational," when as a matter of fact, it was the daily ritual of their addiction.

How did I feel? I was grieved and sickened to see the wasted potential. But I also felt fury. Everything in me wanted to shake them, to say, "Can't you see? Don't you know what you're doing to yourself? You become less and less yourself every time I see you." I wasn't angry because I hated them. I was angry because I cared. If I hadn't loved them, I could have walked away. But love detests what destroys the beloved. Real love stands against the deception, the lie, the sin that destroys. Nearly a century ago the theologian E. H. Gifford wrote, "Human love here offers a true analogy; the more a father loves his son, the more he hates in him the drunkard, the liar, the traitor."

The fact is, anger and love are inseparably bound in human experience. And if I, a flawed person, can feel this much pain and anger over someone else's condition, how much more will the morally perfect God who made them feel pain? If God were not angry over how we are destroying ourselves, he wouldn't be good, and he certainly wouldn't be loving. Anger isn't the opposite of love. Hate is, and the final form of hate is indifference.

Reconciling Justice and Mercy

So we return to our question: how can God execute justice by taking our sin seriously and simultaneously extend mercy and forgiveness? I believe the same conflict between justice and mercy recurs again and again in our own lives. Once in a courtroom, I heard a person being sentenced for a crime. On the one hand, the viewpoint of absolute justice seemed to reign supreme. It was bone chilling to see the impersonal nature of the law. A crime had been committed, and the person had to pay. Justice did not care if the person being tried was someone's son or daughter, sibling or friend. It was irrelevant whether the person was deeply sorry and would clearly never do it again or if he was carrying emotional baggage of his own. He had violated the law. He had to pay.

But another principle and perspective were present in that courtroom. It was almost lost but not quite; it was the law of love. Just as the judge was giving the sentence, a middle-aged man suddenly broke into racking sobs. He was clearly the father of the person on trial, and his anguish changed everything. For a split second we all saw the defendant through a different lens. This was not just a defendant who had committed a crime. This was somebody's child grown up, a child still adored and treasured by a father. Even the judge paused, but he had his job to do and he resumed sentencing. Later, as everyone filed out, I heard the father say, "I have never felt so helpless in my entire life. If only I could have done something. I would have gladly paid the price if I could." That was the first time I had ever been in a courtroom. But the overwhelming memory that I carry with me was not the trial itself but the response of the parent wishing he could have taken the place of his child.

The trouble is, the judge and the father could never be reconciled in their responses to the criminal. The judge would argue, "Unless we clearly condemn evil and show that wrongdoing carries a terrible price, we relegate ourselves to a world of moral chaos." And he would be correct. But what about the father? How can a parent's love ever be silenced in the face of a harsh prison sentence? Many times I have heard older men say, "I really believe in playing hardball with criminal offenders. Some time in the slammer is what they need." Yet if the offender in question is their child, the picture changes entirely—as it should. The judge and the father both have appropriate responses. The judge's job is to sentence. The parent's heart is to stand in for the child.

Stand in for the child? There is our clue. When love comes face-to-face with crisis and suffering in the one who is loved, its first impulse is to stand in, to substitute. Don't we sometimes wish we could bear the suffering of a loved one if it would spare them the trauma? I have never met a parent who did not say of their critically ill child, "How I wish it could have been me instead."

But that is exactly what God felt. *And that is exactly what God did.* He took our place. When the judgment had to fall, he became our substitute, and it fell on him. Only the unthinkable can overcome the irresolvable, and we are left with this remarkable fact: we are the proud sinners, but the final victim of our sin and pride is God. A willing victim. The concept of substitution, or standing in, lies at the heart of the highest love of all and therefore at the heart of our salvation. As John Stott points out in his book *The Cross of Christ:*

For the essence of sin is man substituting himself for God, while the essence of salvation is God substituting himself for man. Man asserts himself against God and puts himself where only God deserves to be; God sacrifices himself for man and puts himself where only man deserves to be. Man claims prerogatives which belong to God alone; God accepts penalties which belong to man alone.

We can be confident of God's love and forgiveness, for in looking at the cross we get our deepest glimpse into the character of God. How can we be sure that God's nature is loving? John Stott continues, "Because the good news of the gospel is that God takes our sinfulness into himself; and overcomes in his own heart what cannot be overcome in human life, since human life remains within the vicious circle of sinful self-glorification on every level of moral advance." God takes evil seriously, but he takes us even more seriously, so that when he judges evil harshly, he sacrifices even his Son to do what it takes to free us. He did not soften his judgment and condemnation of sin. But he let the judgment fall on his Son. That's what substitution means.

The First Step to Freedom

We must own our sin. We live in a therapeutic age

that emphasizes being transparent. But as an astute friend of mine said, "The problem is that transparency hasn't led to transformation—it's led to talk shows." The biblical view is different. We must honestly and humbly confess our sins to God and, when appropriate, to our neighbor. Why? Because as Jesus was crucified for the sin of the world, so must we crucify our own sin. We can't crucify what we refuse to admit. But we don't confess our sins to God or to others in order to prove our authenticity! Rather, we own our sin because that is the only way we can conquer it.

One obstacle that keeps us from being honest about our sins is what I call the "heresy of niceness." Have you ever met a Christian who says, "Now that I know Jesus, I never have a bad day. I never struggle with mixed motives. I just swing from one victory to the next"? Their piety feels more saccharine than sacred. The problem with such otherworldly piety is that it's disengaged from our humanity. It confuses holiness with innocence. Innocence—being free from any taint of sin—was only possible with Adam and Eve before the Fall. The holiness that is possible after the Fall isn't pretending that we have no problems; rather, it's refusing to pretend that we don't. Holiness in light of the cross means we must say, "Lord, though it grieves me to say this, the sin of envy, pride, anger, lust, [you fill in the blank] is exactly the sin I must confess." Ironically, what hinders us most in our pursuit of a godly life is our refusal to admit sin.

I once attended a Bible study with an elderly woman whom I adored but who was definitely of the school of thought that it was a sin to admit she was a sinner. The Bible study leader said, "Why don't we share what one thing controls us that should not." To all of our astonishment she raised her hand and said, "I would like to share the besetting sin of my life: I just don't write enough letters as I should."

Well, all of us certainly felt like sharing our struggles after hearing that riveting confession! I wanted to say to her, "My dear sister, is that why Jesus died? We don't write enough letters? That seems like a stiff price to pay for not having enough stamps."

Another time I heard an evangelist say, "People often say to me, 'Do you ever struggle?' I tell them, 'Maybe I do, maybe I don't, but I'm not going to tell you about it. I just go to God.'" Then he went on to say, "I want to share a poem that I think sums up the Christian life. It's called *Be a Man*:

Feel down, feel discouraged?
   Be a man
Feel like giving up?

Be a man.

Feel like throwing in the towel?

Be a man, be a man, be a man."

Does this poem truly reflect what it means to be a Christian? Is becoming a Christian really making the commitment to never admitting the truth about our weaknesses? I don't recall Jesus saying to the apostle Paul when he was struggling with his thorn in the flesh, "Paul, for crying out loud, would you just buck up and *be a man!* You keep running around sharing this problem. It's so embarrassing. If you can't do better than that, fake it."

No, Jesus said to Paul, "My grace is sufficient for you, for my power is made perfect in weakness" (2 Corinthians 12:9). In other words, "I am glorified in your weakness." In this context Paul is talking about weakness, not sin, but the principle is the same: we must own our sin and bring it to God so that we can overcome it, and in doing so, God can be glorified.

The cross frees us to own our sin. And the cross reminds us that we cannot overcome what we refuse to admit.

Perhaps you are reading this, and you know you have never confessed to God your sin of self-rule. You know that Jesus has not been the Lord of your life. You want to give your life to Christ, but you don't know how.

Rick's story. A few years ago I boarded a plane and took my seat next to a man who appeared to be in his late twenties or early thirties. I had just finished speaking at a conference, and all I wanted was to sit quietly and read my book. But my seatmate, who soon introduced himself as Rick, seemed eager to talk. As I put my book away, I asked him what he did for a living.

He told me he had been a rather famous race-car driver. In his racing days he thought he had everything: fame, money, all the trappings of success. He felt invulnerable. That all ended when he was in a near-fatal car accident while driving in a race. He was hospitalized for months, his worst injury being severely broken legs. After a long period of therapy and an extended stay at the hospital, he was finally released. Remarkably, he was able to walk without a limp, but his doctors told him he could never race again.

Without his career or a big income to give him identity, he became terribly depressed. He had been a heavy drinker before, but now he became a full-fledged alcoholic. Looking back, he said there were four or five years that he couldn't even account for. Then one night, in a drunken stupor, he crashed his car into a wall. For weeks the doctors didn't think he would live, but amazingly he pulled through. When he was fully conscious, he was informed that both legs had been broken again. He was told he would probably never walk. He knew he'd come to the end of his rope.

Rick said, "I've never been a religious person, but for the first time in my life, I cried out to God and asked him to help me. I told him I was sorry I'd made such a mess of my life. I asked God to please let me walk again. I promised that as soon as I was released, I would join Alcoholics Anonymous. I also told God that I'd try to find out more about him so we could get to know each other."

Sure enough, to the astonishment of his doctors, after extensive therapy, his severely broken bones mended, the connective tissues healed and once again he was able to walk. He kept his word, and on being released from the hospital he joined Alcoholic Anonymous. He hadn't had a drop to drink for sixteen months. Not only that, but at the AA meetings he had met a wonderful woman whom he planned to marry soon.

We talked for a long time about the changes in his life, his goals and dreams for the future, and his profound regrets about the people he had hurt during his alcoholic days. What haunted him most was that he had never visited his beloved grandfather while the old man lay dying of cancer in the hospital. His grandfather died while Rick was still in an alcoholic haze; he never got to say goodbye.

Then I said, "You know, Rick, the pain of facing your regrets now that you are sober is tough. It's very tough. But I must tell you how much I admire your courage in facing yourself, for owning your problem and sticking with your recovery. I think owning our problems is the hardest work any of us has to do. It's hard on our pride, but ultimately it is liberating, don't you agree?"

"No question about it. The hardest part was to stop blaming everybody else and accept responsibility for what was my problem alone. But you're right—it was freeing to finally own it. Becky, you really seem to understand, and you don't feel judgmental. Hey, are you in recovery too?" he asked with sudden intensity.

I paused for several seconds before answering. "Yes, I am in recovery. But not from alcohol. I'm in recovery for a problem far deeper than alcoholism."

"What do you mean?" Rick asked as his eyes widened.

"I'm in recovery, Rick, from what the Bible calls sin. You know why I don't seem judgmental to you? Because I've learned that the only thing that separates people is their symptoms, but *all* of us suffer from the same underlying disease of sin. It's the one disease everyone needs recovery from."

"I'm not sure I get it. What's the difference between being a drunk and being a sinner? Isn't it the same thing?" Rick asked.

"Alcoholism is the addictive behavior. Sin is what lurks behind the behavior. The *core* of sin isn't so much a set of behaviors as it is having a God-complex. You could never drink a drop of alcohol again, Rick, and still be determined to run your own life rather than let God be in charge. Sin is choosing to be self-ruled instead of God-ruled. And destructive behavior, in whatever form it takes, is always the inevitable result of refusing to let God be God."

"Oh, man, I can really identify with what you're saying. I took such pride in being in charge of my life. No one—not God, not my parents—*no one* could tell me what to do. And look at where it got me! But if AA is the treatment for alcoholism, then what's the treatment for sin?" Rick asked.

"Let me ask you something, Rick. You said that you cried out to God in the hospital. Now you follow the twelve-step program, which means you daily acknowledge your powerlessness over your addiction, which you can't conquer without the help of a 'Higher Power,' right?"

"Absolutely!"

"Have you found the name for this 'Higher Power'?"

"No, not yet," Rick answered. "But ever since I

prayed that night in the hospital, my life has been different. I can just tell God has been looking out for me. I'm still searching, though. I want to know more about who God is."

"Rick, I know the name of the Higher Power. His name is Jesus. And the treatment for sin is the cross. All of us have tried to live our lives as if we deserved to be God, and look at the mess we've created! But God sent his Son, Jesus, who took our broken humanity into himself and made it his own. We deserved God's judgment, but Jesus stepped in and took it for us. He sacrificed his life for us and overcame our sin in his own heart so that *our* hearts could be changed. He rose from the dead, and he offers to heal our brokenness, to forgive our sins and to make us whole. We just need to surrender our lives to him, to repent and believe."

"Yeah, but I've blown it so bad. I mean, I know God is there; otherwise, I'd probably be dead by now. But how could I ever believe that God would forgive me for everything? Especially after all that I've done, it just wouldn't seem fair."

"That's what the cross is all about, Rick! All of us nailed Jesus to the cross. Alcoholics and teetotalers, church folk and pagans, preachers and prostitutes—all of us are responsible for the death of Jesus. But Jesus loved us so much that he voluntarily chose to die for us. Don't you see, Rick, if the cross shows us how serious our sin is, it also shows us that there is nothing we could ever do that cannot be forgiven."

"You think your sins are bad," I continued, "but have you ever considered that you've done something worse than being an alcoholic? You are responsible for the death of God's Son. And so am I. Our insistence on playing God is what drove Jesus to the cross. What could be worse than that? And if the cross shows us that God is willing to forgive us for the death of his Son, then why wouldn't he be willing to forgive us for every other sin? That's the amazing love of the cross."

Rick was a strong, rough-hewed kind of guy. But for the first time in our two-hour plane ride, he wept. Unbeknownst to me, Rick had boarded our plane with a heart that God had been preparing for a long time. All he needed was to hear the proclamation of the gospel. He was wide open and ready to receive Jesus as Lord. As our plane touched down, he asked me how to make a confession of faith. Then he bowed his head in silence for several minutes.

Afterward he said, "Listen, my fiancée will be waiting for me outside. I'd really like for her to meet you. I want to share everything we've talked about with her. And I'd like to start our marriage together in faith. Do you have any suggestions?"

"Well, start by sharing with her what has just happened to you. And may I be the first to send you a wedding present? I'd love to give you a family Bible and a devotional book that you can read together. And I'll send a book on the basics of the Christian faith. Okay?"

It was a small airport, and as we quickly reached the waiting area, his fiancée was there. Rick introduced me and began to excitedly tell her everything we had talked about. She looked slightly dazed by his overwhelming enthusiasm, but I couldn't stay to help explain. Since I knew someone was waiting to pick me up, I excused myself and started walking across the airport.

Then I realized someone was calling my name. It was Rick's fiancée, calling me from the other side of the waiting area. By the look on her face it was clear that Rick had told her about his new-found faith. With tears streaming down her cheeks, she shouted across a crowded airport, "Becky, thank you! Thank you! Thank you!"

I cannot imagine a more theologically appropriate benediction to that experience. What else can we say in response to a God of such generosity, such love, such grace, who pardons our sins when we deserve death, who transforms us, fills us with his Spirit and delights to call us his own?

The longer I live, the more I have come to see that the only language appropriate for such an awesome God is the response of praise overflowing from a grateful heart—praise that says in awe and humility, "Oh, God, thank you! Thank you! Thank you!"

Rick had felt a great deal of guilt for his alcoholism. Ironically, what set him free was looking at the cross and realizing that the core of his problem was much deeper than simply taking another drink. The cross always brings us out of hiding because it makes us see that if Jesus had to die, then we have a problem that is far more serious than we ever imagined. Yet the cross also gives us hope. The cross breaks our denial, but only *in the very instant* that it shows us the possibility of forgiveness. It shows us our corruption, but in the same breath it tells us the price has been paid.

The Christian view of sin is radical but not pessimistic because to see sin in Christian terms is to see that sin can be forgiven. That really is freedom. That really is amazing grace.

The Second Step to Freedom

We are free to love the unlovely. If the first lesson from the cross is that we must own our problem, then the second lesson from the cross is that we are free to love the unlovely. What I love about the cross is that it is so democratic. All of us suffer from the same disease; we are all healed by the same cure. The ground is level at the cross. The cross makes racism an impossibility. And it means that a Christian can never pull away from somebody who is not a believer and say, "I cannot possibly relate to him. She's not a believer! They're not good enough!"

Helen's story. Several years ago I became friends with Helen. She has a larger-than-life temperament and is very bright, quite sensitive and has almost no church background. In fact, she was quite worldly.

One day she said to me, "Becky, my husband is very intrigued that I have a friend who is a Christian, and he wants to meet you." So the three of us arranged to have lunch together.

At one point during lunch her husband said, "I just want to say one thing, Becky. We are not religious." This was not a news flash. I had figured that out all by myself. He went on to say, "We have what I call an open marriage." (I remember thinking, *I don't know what it is, but it sure sounds like sin to me.*) He said, "She has her affairs; I have mine. It's the modern age after all."

As we walked out of the restaurant, my friend turned to me and said, "The truth is, I don't have many affairs. I have one. I am madly in love with another man. I want to marry him; I want to leave my husband. But I have little children, and I don't know what to do." From that point on when we met, she'd share the pain and the agony of the choices before her.

To love people as Jesus calls us to is never easy or tidy. But God will help us as we seek to love wisely and well. I asked the Lord if even listening to her talk about her affair gave the false impression that I condoned it. What I felt God saying to me in my spirit was, "Becky, let her know that what she wants is absolutely right. She's looking for love, she's looking for wholeness, she's looking for healing. But she's looking in all the places that will destroy her." I told her what God had impressed on my spirit.

I had asked her many times to read the Bible. But she always assured me she had no interest whatsoever. Then one day to my astonishment she said, "I have a question for you. In the Gospel of Mark . . ."

Overjoyed, I said, "I knew it! I knew if I mentioned it enough you would finally read the Bible!"

"Oh, you had nothing to do with it," she said. "I was with my lover the other day and he asked me, 'What do you think about Jesus?'"

She replied to her lover, "Pardon me?"

He said, "Well, I've never read the New Testament, so I thought I would, and I can't get over Jesus. I can't get over how beautiful and powerful he is. I went to others and asked them to tell me more about Jesus, but they were not much help. So I thought maybe you know something and could help me."

Helen replied, "Oh, I'm terribly sorry. I take all of my religious questions to Becky." Then she gave me a list of all the questions her lover had. She told me that the next time she and her lover got together, among other things, they were going to do a Bible study in Mark.

Now I have heard of unusual contexts for Bible study, but I thought this must take first prize. I told Helen, "If you're finally going to read the Bible, then do it with me first." That's how we began to read the Bible together.

Our first Bible study was at her place, and by now we'd become really good friends. I handed her a Bible, told her what page to turn to, and as we were reading along I began to sense that she was uncomfortable. Suddenly she put her hands over the Bible and said in almost a whisper, "May I ask you a personal question?"

"Yes," I replied.

"Do you think the Bible would object if I had a little glass of wine?" she asked.

I said, "Well, why don't you ask it? No, I'm kidding. Listen, this is your home. I want you to be comfortable." So she got a glass of wine. A little bit later, with her hands over the Bible again (presumably so the Bible wouldn't hear!), she said, "Do you think there would be any objection if I smoke a little cigarillo? I'm very nervous."

From that point on we met every week. She had a glass of wine in one hand and a cigarillo in another, and we read about Jesus. She would take what we studied and share it with her lover a few days later.

One day Helen and I were reading about the prostitute at Simon's banquet. I noticed that her eyes grew wider and wider. "Becky," she said, "all my life I have felt that I am worth about as much as a piece of dirt. I'm so lost. I thought that if there was a God, he despised my lostness. But according to this, if you're lost, Jesus loves you. Even more amazing than that, if you're lost and you know you're lost, you are probably close to the kingdom of God. Can you imagine me close to the kingdom of God?"

"Oh yes," I said, "I can imagine it very easily." Tears welled up in my eyes as I tried to explain. "Do you know what has happened to you? You have seen the real Jesus. That doesn't make you a Christian yet, but once you've glimpsed Jesus as he really is, it's hard to stay the same."

After that Bible study, there were significant changes. Helen broke off the relationship with her lover. She told him, "I'm trying to find out if Jesus is God. If he is, then I'm sure our affair wouldn't be pleasing to him. This may be the biggest mistake I have ever made. But if Jesus is who he says he is, then it will have been worth the risk."

Two weeks later her husband received a job transfer to a foreign country. They left within three weeks. I was heartsick that she left before becoming a Christian. Furthermore, she was going to a country where Christianity could not be openly practiced. Before she left I gave her a Bible and told her I would be praying daily for her. In the meantime, her lover called me and asked where he could go to get his spiritual questions answered. He was a genuine seeker, and I put him in touch with a Christian man.

One month later I received a transatlantic telephone call. My friend said, "Becky, I've got to tell you something. You aren't going to believe this, but I met this man and his wife at an open-air market, and it turns out they are Christians! I don't know what it is, but they have an aroma that just smells like you. Not only that, but he's the pastor of a church. I'm actually going to church!"

Then she said, "One last thing, I've been reading the Bible every day to my five-year-old son.

One day I told him, 'You know, Mommy is trying to find out if Jesus is God. I want to believe, but it's hard.' Becky, my son answered, 'Oh Mommy! I know Jesus. Since you've been reading to me about him, he comes to me and talks to me. Mommy, Jesus is my best friend.'"

As I listened to her with tears streaming down my face, I could only think, *What kind of God is this? A God who goes to an adulterous bed, where people in their blindness and lostness are breaking sacred vows, hurting children they don't intend to hurt.* Yet Jesus comes to them and says, "Give me a chance. I love you. I'm really what you're looking for. Give your brokenness to me." That the universe could contain a God of such generosity makes me want to rise and sing the doxology! "While we were still sinners, Christ died for us" (Romans 5:8).

Right before she hung up she said, "Becky, I want so much to believe, it's just so hard to believe there is an invisible Father in heaven who could love me, when my earthly experience has been so difficult. But I believe one day I will find him."

Why do I have the freedom to love Helen deeply? Made in the image of God, we share a common humanity. But deeper still, the cross shows me I'm no different. Do you think it matters to Jesus that my list of sins is not the same as hers? Mine cost Jesus his life just as hers did. That is why we can reach out to those around us with outstretched arms. We do so out of sheer gratitude for what God has done for us—and because we know that if he can change us, he can change anybody. In one way, the cross divides. It draws a line across history. It stands between good and evil, truth and lies. But in another way it unites. The cross is the leveling ground on which differences of status, success and character are swallowed up before a judgment and a mercy that exclude no one.

◆　◆　◆

The story of Helen happened sixteen years ago. Over those years she experienced some great difficulties that caused her to give up her search for God. I was grieved to hear that she had turned her back on faith. Nevertheless, I prayed.

Then from out of the blue I received an e-mail from her two years ago. After catching me up on her past, which included telling me that her now-grown son was a true believer, she wrote, "But this you must know—thanks to endless discussions with my son, my indebtedness to your original witness and the ever-patient love and consistent example of our dear mutual friend—I have at last finally succumbed to his grace. I was lost but now I'm found; was blind but now I see."

The Bible tells us that "the Lord . . . is patient

with you, not wanting anyone to perish, but everyone to come to repentance" (2 Peter 3:9). Helen's conversion reminded me once again that all is grace—whether it takes fourteen years or forty.

The Way of Jesus

So what did I say to my Harvard professor when he told me, "You've proven to me that Jesus really doesn't make a difference"?

I told him, "You know, a minute ago you just swore and then you said, 'Oh, excuse me, Becky, I'm so sorry I forgot.'" I said, "It's a kind gesture, but isn't the thought behind it due to the fact that I'm a Christian, and therefore I'm innocent, and your job is to protect me from the big bad world out there?"

He laughed and said, "That's exactly what I was thinking."

I said, "Well, excuse me for being so direct, sir, but you are the perceived innocent, not me. You see, I'm a follower of Jesus, and he has shown me that I am not innocent and never was. If all that's wrong with us is that we occasionally use colorful language, then we are in pretty good shape. No, walking with Jesus has enabled me to see my problem—it's called sin."

He said, "Golly, and you seemed so nice to me."

I said, "But don't you see, that's where the true

difference that Jesus makes begins to reveal itself. Jesus helps me see and own what's wrong with me!"

My professor replied, "But you're so joyful. If I was that hard on myself, I'd be so depressed."

"Oh, but Jesus hasn't just given us the diagnosis of the problem," I replied. "He's given us the cure. The cure is his forgiveness of our sins, his presence with us through his Spirit and the power to walk in the Spirit and not the flesh."

"Has the cure worked?" he asked.

"Yes, it is working. I am learning how to live in recovery from sin, and I am growing in amazing grace. And you're right—it does make me joyful," I explained.

What is the final fruit of the cross? It is joy. As G. K. Chesterton has written in his book *Orthodoxy*, "Joy, which was the small publicity of the pagan, is the gigantic secret of the Christian."

Questions to Ponder or Discuss

1. What have you understood about the cross in a fresh way from reading this book?

2. According to the author, in order to understand the mystery and the miracle of radical change that Jesus offers, what must we first face (pp. 8-10)?

3. On page 21 the author defines *sin* as having a God-complex that leaves us addicted to ourselves. What do you think of this?

4. We live in a culture that says the way to be happy is to think only positive thoughts. But the author says that in order to experience true joy we must first face the mess of the human heart. How can facing the problem help?

5. Why do you think many of us resist facing our mess?

6. Like the gospel, psychology tells us to face our problems. But the cross goes further, telling us to face God as well. It shows us that our problem is worse than we thought and God's solution is far more magnificent than we imagined. How would a person's life be different if he or she really believed these truths?

7. How can Christ's death make a difference in the way we live?

Other books by Rebecca Manley Pippert

Hope Has Its Reasons

This is a book geared for people who want honest answers to honest questions. The author examines the persistently human longings that all of us share about significance, meaning, life and truth, and the search for security. Only after she unravels the core of the real problem that plagues us does she explore how Christ can meet our longings and solve our human crisis. There are no canned formulas or saccharine clichés. Realism rings in the stories she tells and the ideas she pursues. In doing so she leads us beyond the search for our own significance to the reasons for our hope in discovering God. *197 pp., 2278-X*

A Heart for God

How can God use the difficulties and sufferings in our lives to build character and deepen our faith? The biblical David faced some desperate circumstances and some tough choices. So do we, day by day. The author shows us how God is able to use the everyday grit and glory of our lives to shape a holy life within us. Using David as her guide she helps us understand the way Christian virtue is developed in our souls and vices are rooted out. We learn how we, like David, can choose the good, overcome temptation and grow to be one who has a heart for God. *236 pp., 2341-7*

Transformation

Would you like to move from despair to hope? Would you like to transform your feelings of fear to faith? Would you like to turn envy into compassion? The Bible shows how David turned these negative emotions in his life into godly character qualities. In this Christian Basics Bible Study, based on the Bible's account of David and the book *A Heart for God,* you'll investigate David's life, choices, mistakes and triumphs. Then you'll discover how you can make the same transformation in your own life. *6 studies, 2019-1*